Lerner SPORTS

EXTREME SPEED

SUPERFAST
DRAG
RACING

J Chris Roselius

Lerner Publications ◆ Minneapolis

Lerner Publications Company
An imprint of Lerner Publishing Group, Inc.
241 First Avenue North
Minneapolis, MN 55401 USA

For reading levels and more information, look up this title at www.lernerbooks.com.

Main body text set in Myriad Pro.
Typeface provided by Adobe.

Library of Congress Cataloging-in-Publication Data

Names: Roselius, J Chris, author.
Title: Superfast drag racing / by J Chris Roselius.
Description: Minneapolis : Lerner Publications, 2020. | Series: Extreme speed | Includes bibliographical references and index. | Audience: Ages 7–11 | Audience: Grades 2–3 | Summary: "Start your engines and get in gear! Full-color photos and engaging text will have readers turning the pages to discover the history of drag racing, what a typical race day looks like, and more"— Provided by publisher.
Identifiers: LCCN 2019026106 (print) | LCCN 2019026107 (ebook) | ISBN 9781541577190 (hardcover) | ISBN 9781541587359 (paperback) | ISBN 9781541582903 (ebook)
Subjects: LCSH: Drag racing—Juvenile literature. | Dragsters—Juvenile literature.
Classification: LCC GV1029.3 .R67 2020 (print) | LCC GV1029.3 (ebook) | DDC 796.72—dc23

LC record available at https://lccn.loc.gov/2019026106
LC ebook record available at https://lccn.loc.gov/2019026107

Manufactured in the United States of America
1 – CG – 12/31/19

CONTENTS

CHAPTER 1

DOMINATING THE STRIP

Drag racing cars burst off the starting line with amazing speeds.

It was late October in 2018, and the crowd at the Las Vegas Motor Speedway stood in anticipation. Their eyes were on the drivers, Steve Torrence and Richie Crampton. Many people at the track wondered about Torrence. Would he finally win his first National Hot Rod Association (NHRA) Mello Yello Drag Racing Series Top Fuel championship?

- In 2018, Steve Torrence became the first driver to win every race of the Countdown since the six-race playoff format started in 2007.

- Top Fuel dragsters race at 330 miles (530 km) per hour.

- Top Fuel dragsters cover the 1,000-foot (300 m) track in 3.7 seconds.

- Drag racing cars can reach noise levels between 125 and 150 decibels. This is similar to the sound of a jet taking off and is loud enough to damage someone's ears.

Each car has its own lane during drag races.

The NHRA Countdown to the Championship is a six-race playoff that determines the sport's champion. It begins after the eighteenth race of the Top Fuel season, with the top ten drivers in each classification earning a spot in the six-race playoff. Drivers earn points during the season and compete in the playoffs based on where they finish in each event. They also earn performance bonus points during each qualifying session.

Torrence won the first four Championship events in 2018. All he needed now was to win the **elimination** semifinal race to give him enough points to win his first title. Then, no other driver could earn enough points to beat him, not even in the final Championship race.

The finish line was only 1,000 feet (300 m) away from the start. Inching his car forward until he was **staged** at the starting line, Torrence concentrated on the starting lights—known as the Christmas tree—in order to get the best start possible. When the light turned green, Torrence burst away from the starting line. In less than four seconds, after reaching speeds of 330 miles (480 km) per hour, he beat Crampton to the finish line.

PRESTAGE

STAGE

DRAG RACING CHRONO

The Christmas tree tells drag racers when to cross the starting line.

The crowd cheered. Torrence was the new champion! Two weeks later, he won the NHRA Auto Club event in Pomona, California. By beating Tony Schumacher in the finals, Torrence became the first driver to win every race of the Countdown since the six-race playoff format started in 2007.

The NHRA is the top drag racing circuit in the United States. Drag racing gained popularity in the early 1930s. People would race in the dry lake beds in the Mojave Desert in California. Wally Parks, the editor for *Hot Rod* magazine at the time, formed the NHRA and created safety rules and standards in 1951. The first NHRA race was held in April 1953 in Pomona. Since then, the NHRA has grown to include 40,000 licensed competitors who compete on more than 120 tracks in the United States.

Drag racers can technically win the Championship before the final race based on how many points they earn during the season.

CHAPTER 2

DRAG RACING CARS

Top Fuel cars have long, sleek designs.

Dragsters often produce flames as they speed down the track.

The NHRA sanctions over 200 different drag racing classes at its events. At most NHRA events, the top four classes are Top Fuel, Funny Car, Pro Stock, and Pro Stock Motorcycles.

Top Fuel dragsters and Funny Cars have engines that run on a special fuel called **nitromethane**. This fuel produces a lot more power than gasoline. Because this fuel is so powerful and dangerous, these races are capped at a distance of 1,000 feet (300 m). The tracks also have longer areas at the end to slow down cars. This helps keep drivers safe. Most other drag races cover 1,320 feet (402 m), which is 0.25 miles (0.4 km).

Each drag racing class has a different type of engine. These powerful engines are maintained by the pit crew.

Top Fuel dragsters race at 330 miles (530 km) per hour and can cover the track in 3.7 seconds. The engines can generate 10,000 horsepower and burn 15 gallons (57 L) of nitromethane fuel in a single race. The cars, which are 25 feet (7.6 m) long, must weigh at least 2,330 pounds (1,056 kg) including the driver.

Funny Cars use the same type of engine as Top Fuel dragsters and can reach similar speeds. They cover the track in an average of 3.8 seconds. However, Funny Cars are much shorter and heavier, weighing at least 2,555 pounds (1,160 kg) with the driver. Funny Cars got their name because of how they look. All four of a Funny Car's wheels are set more forward on the car's **chassis**. This makes them look different than Top Fuel cars, and some think the design is "funny."

REALLY?!

When it comes to Top Fuel and Funny Car racing, one of the highest costs for teams is the fuel they buy. Drag racers can burn 1.2 gallons (4.5 L) of nitromethane per second. In 2018, a 42-gallon (159 L) drum of nitromethane cost $1,428.

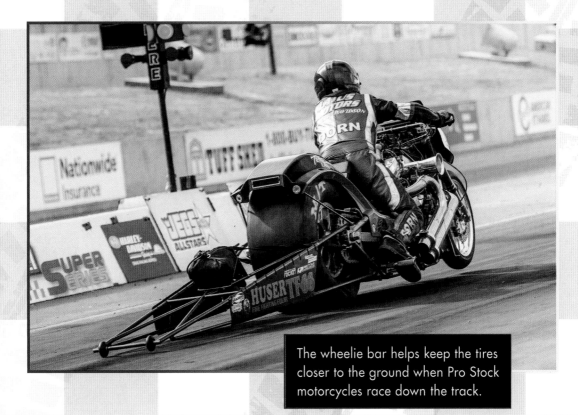

The wheelie bar helps keep the tires closer to the ground when Pro Stock motorcycles race down the track.

Pro Stock cars look like most cars on the road. They must weigh 2,350 pounds (1,066 kg) with the driver. They can go faster than 210 miles (338 km) per hour and race down the track in 6.5 seconds. Pro Stock motorcycles look very different from regular motorcycles. Their many modifications include a wheelie bar that extends behind the bike. This helps the bike maintain balance. They can reach speeds close to 200 miles (322 km) per hour and cover the track in 6.8 seconds.

Top Fuel dragsters, Funny Cars, and Pro Stock cars and motorcycles are expensive. The giant rear wheels used by dragsters and Funny Cars cost $1,100 per pair. Drag racing vehicles range in cost from $180,000 for a Top Fuel dragster to $250,000 for a Pro Stock car, though the costs vary from team to team.

Dragsters slow down using parachutes.

CHAPTER 3

DRIVERS AND CREW

In 2018,
Leah Pritchett
competed for two
NHRA titles.

Competing in a drag race takes amazing skill. It requires drivers to be in top physical condition. Drivers work out regularly to get stronger and stay in shape.

Leah Pritchett has ten career wins and has reached a speed of just over 334 miles (538 km) per hour in her Top Fuel dragster. Pritchett believes her success on the track is related to her fitness. Throughout the week, Pritchett eats a healthy diet and strengthens her core muscles, arms, and legs through different types of exercises. She also does a lot of cardiovascular exercises such as jogging and sprints.

On race day, drivers go through pre-race routines. Racers grab their gear, head to the **staging lanes**, and drink water. They also put in mouthpieces to avoid chipping their teeth during the race.

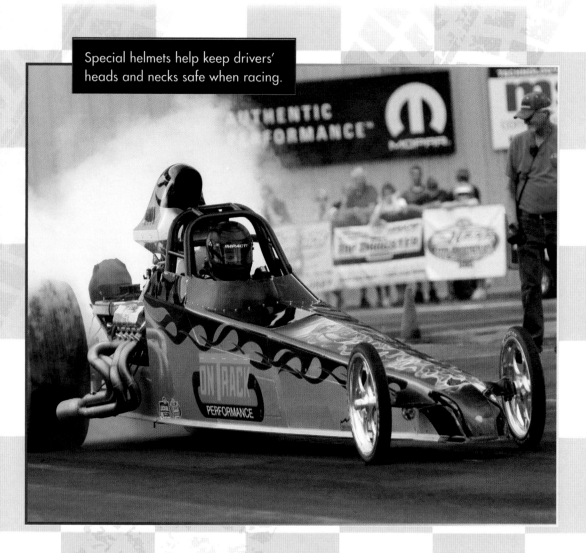

Special helmets help keep drivers' heads and necks safe when racing.

Heating and cleaning the tires before every race is important.

After putting on the helmet, a driver's pit crew helps him or her get into a firesuit, a neck collar for the **HANS device**, and a pair of gloves. The driver straps into the seat with a shoulder harness. He or she then flips on the ignition switch to the car and slowly heads to the **water box**, where the driver does a **burnout** to heat up and clean the tires.

While the driver prepares for the race, the pit crew is busy working on the car. Seven to nine people work in each pit crew. The crew chief runs the show and assigns each task to be done. Pit crews also have a co-crew chief and specialized technicians. The crew chief makes final decisions about the car.

The pit crew is vital to the success of a driver. They are the experts who make sure the car is running as well as it can. The crew also ensures that the cars drive as safely as possible. The entire team works together to keep a driver safe on race day.

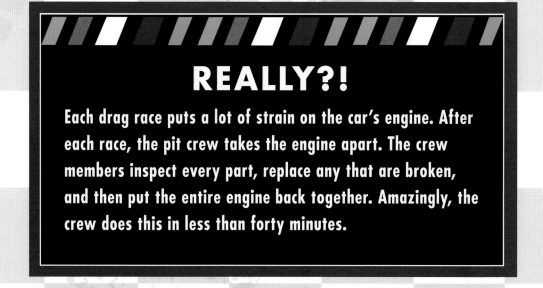

REALLY?!

Each drag race puts a lot of strain on the car's engine. After each race, the pit crew takes the engine apart. The crew members inspect every part, replace any that are broken, and then put the entire engine back together. Amazingly, the crew does this in less than forty minutes.

Each person on the pit crew has a specific task for each race.

Racers travel to drag events around the country during the NHRA season.

Drag races can happen during the day or night.

Many tracks around the United States host drag racing events. One of the most famous tracks is Auto Club Raceway at Pomona, California. The first NHRA sanctioned event was held at the Auto Club Raceway in 1953. In 1961, the track was the site of the first NHRA Winternationals race, the opening race of the NHRA season. Pomona has hosted the event every year since.

At the Gainesville Raceway, fans view the racing action from metal bleachers.

Other famous tracks include Lucas Oil Raceway in Indiana, the Gainesville Raceway in Florida, and the Bristol Dragway in Tennessee. Each track has a long history with drag racing. Fans have watched drag races at the tracks for many decades.

Earplugs are very important for people who attend drag races. Cars launching down the runway can reach noise levels between 125 and 150 decibels. This is close to the level of sound of a jet taking off and is loud enough to damage someone's ears.

Both fans and racing officials wear ear protection during drag races.

PROFILE IN SPEED

DON GARLITS. Don Garlits, known as "Big Daddy" to his fans, is called by some the "Father of Drag Racing." Garlits started drag racing after World War II. He won a total of 144 events and seventeen titles— ten American Hot Rod Association titles, four International Hot Rod Association championships, and three National Hot Rod Association titles. In 1987, his Top Fuel dragster Swamp Rat XXX was enshrined in the National Museum of American History in Washington, DC.

Spectators can also visit the pit area on race day. There they can stand close to drivers and mechanics before the race begins. They may even get an autograph from their favorite driver.

Though drag racing is traditionally dominated by male drivers, many women have been successful in drag racing. In 1965, Shirley Muldowney became the first woman to earn a **competition license** and race in an NHRA event. Today, Brittany Force and Leah Pritchett are two of the best Top Fuel drivers.

On race day, drag fans can get close to the large rear tires in the pit area.

Don Garlits visits drag racing conventions to meet with fans.

Drag may soon feature electric vehicles. As of 2019, electric cars could not reach the same speeds as Top Fuel dragsters or Funny Cars. According to the National Electric Drag Racing Association, the record for an electric dragster on the 0.25-mile (402 m) course is 7.274 seconds, with the car going 185 miles (298 km) per hour. This record was set by Don Garlits. Thanks to constant improvement in technology, it may not be long before electric cars are capable of going as fast as the top cars in the NHRA. The future of drag racing is unknown, but it is exciting.

DRAG RACING
FAMILY TREE

Drag racing has changed a lot over the years, but one thing has remained the same—the cars are made to go fast!

Don Westerdale, 1960s

Don "The Snake" Prudhomme, 1970s

Mike Dun, 1990s

Brittany Force, 2010s

GLOSSARY

burnout
spinning of rear wheels in water to heat and clean the tires before a race

chassis
the body of a car that other parts attach to

competition license
a license needed to compete in NHRA sanctioned events. Drivers must be at least eighteen years old to get a pro competition license.

elimination
a style of race where cars compete two at a time. The winner continues to race in the competition, while the loser is done.

HANS device
a safety device worn around the driver's shoulders that helps protect the head and neck during a crash

nitromethane
a fuel used specifically for drag racing. It is the result of a chemical reaction between nitric acid and propane.

staged
when the front wheels of the race car are on the starting line

staging lanes
an area in a race facility that leads to the racing surface, where cars are lined up and paired before making a run

water box
where vehicles and motorcycles start their burnouts to clean and heat up their tires

FURTHER INFORMATION

Adamson, Thomas K. *Dragsters*. Minneapolis: Bellwether, 2019.

Bell, Samantha S. *Building Race Cars*. Lake Elmo, MN: Focus Readers, 2018.

Chicagoland Speedway: Drag Racing 101
http://www.kidsclubracing.com/Racing-101/Drag-Racing-101.aspx

Junior Drag Racing League
http://jrdragster.nhra.com/leagueracer-info/about-the-jdrl

Monnig, Alex. *Behind the Wheel of a Dragster*. Mankato, MN: Child's World, 2016.

National Hot Rod Association
https://www.nhra.com/nhra

INDEX

PHOTO ACKNOWLEDGMENTS

The images in this book are used with the permission of: © Action Sports Photography/Shutterstock.com, pp. 4, 10, 15, 24; ©: Phillip Rubino/Shutterstock.com, pp. 5, 14, 18, 19, 22; ©: Robert Young/Shutterstock.com, p. 6; ©: DenisVolkov/Shutterstock.com, p. 7; ©: Will Lester/Digital First Media/Inland Valley Daily Bulletin/MediaNews Group/Getty Images, pp. 8–9; ©: Michael Stokes/Shutterstock.com, p. 11; ©: Ken Morris/Shutterstock.com, p. 12; Matthew Bolt/Icon Sportswire/Getty Images, pp. 16, 29 (bottom right); ©: BoJack/Shutterstock.com, p. 17; ©: Steve Mann/Shutterstock.com, p. 21; ©: Andy Cross/The Denver Post/Getty Images, pp. 23, 29 (bottom left); ©: Stephen Mcsweeny/Shutterstock.com, p. 25; ©: ©: Steve Lagreca/Shutterstock.com, pp. 26, 28; Divin Serhiy/Shutterstock.com, p. 27; ©: Pat Brollier/The Enthusiast Network/Getty Images, p. 29 (top left); ©: Craig Cutler/The Enthusiast Network/Getty Images, p. 29 (top right).

Front Cover: ©: Tony Watson/Alamy.